American Dervish
STEVEN REESE

For Brian & Judy,
amidst the stormy
Synchronicities of Boston,
March 2013 —
with great affection,
Steve

salmonpoetry

Published in 2013 by
Salmon Poetry
Cliffs of Moher, County Clare, Ireland
Website: www.salmonpoetry.com
Email: info@salmonpoetry.com

ISBN 978-1-908836-47-2

COVER ARTWORK: *"Surgery" by Mary K. Farragher*
COVER DESIGN: *Siobhán Hutson*

Printed in Ireland by Sprint Print

This book, for Kelly

Acknowledgments

Grateful acknowledgment is extended to the following publications in which these poems originally appeared:

Artful Dodge: "His Preference for Winter"

Asheville Review: "Dead Letter to a Special Agent"

Boxcar Review: "Nearer the Truth"

Diode: "Bad Magic"

Florida Review: "American Legend"

Green Mountains Review: "The Death of Orpheus"

Hurricane Review: "Dervish for Mike Fink, Alligator-Horse"

The Journal: "Dervish," "Dervish for Annie Oakley," "Our Ships," "Snow Day," "When She Was Gone"

Massachusetts Review: "The First Translation"

Midwest Quarterly: "Practice Elegy for My Father"

Poet Lore: "Hans Asperger and the Bomb," "Ben's Scripts"

Poetry Northwest: "Bruxism," "Proposing to the Widow DeWine," "One Hallow's E'en," "Seeing You," "From the Top of Mt. Wrightson," "Snap the Whip"

Roanoke Review: "Lindsay's Dervish"

Slant: "Ohio's 200th Birthday Dervish"

Southeast Review: "Cold"

Tar River Poetry: "Small Ode to My Ignorance"

West Branch: "Tour Guide, Fallingwater," "Tent"

Contents

III: If You Lived Here

I
Dervishes

Dervish

Our history personified might begin
as that B western scene where the liquored-up villain
pulls six-shooters, says *dance,*
and starts blasting the ground out from under our feet—

we're pressed into it,
              this hide-saving highstep
        improvised *in extremis,* this whirling
that goes on even after the shooting stops

until it leaps clear of that genre
altogether
                and becomes something other,
        a part of our character, a species
of pleasure that takes to the woods,
to the maypole, won't hold to one key or measure,
it wanders us

              west of ourselves, into
        a way of knowing, an identity, almost
an art,
but Toqueville says no, not an art, we can't
really dance, and he's right, he's French, look
how we blunder and knock over chairs and dance
over graves without thinking,
              it's half compulsion still,
        we hardly know

how to describe it when that dancing master,
John Chapman, lugs his seed-sack

through the Seven Ranges, solitary, sleeps with
                    snakes and savages, spouts
            Swedenborg to trees
and turns a nice little profit, too—look at him, the man's
thinking cap's a kettle, what do we call that,
the birth of pragmatism? some other shufflestep?

And we half
                    hate ourselves for it and for not
            dancing like Europe and
for trying the whole time to do it in shackles, till we
dance ourselves dead into corners, into boxes
like bleeding Kansas, and have
                    to fight our way out
            of ourselves, beat
each other blue and gray till we know it's for real,
not just bluster and Barnum and Many-fest Dance-ity

but the smallest nerves, too,
                    that leap in a President's brain
            when the bullet enters, the last neurons'
skip-kick like Annie Oakley's after her curtain-call
bullseye, it's all too much to fall

under any one name, too big and too small, profit
                    and poetry, tall-tale canon-thunder
            iron rails touching
two shores but
then Whitman's touch, too, in the hospitals,
and that other railroad, the night train, underground,
slipping through woods, not

only Sam Houston's barrel of bourbon a day
but Emerson's "tipsy on water,"
and our new
                    colossus no giant at all but a mother
            of exiles, and they

flock to her, fling themselves into the dance,
change it, speed it, give it our stamp and stomp,
round
                        and round and on, so vast
              and junk-cluttered we're apt
to be lost in it
or sit it out or wave a flag and say

it's only a march, always has been, nothing fancy, no
finesse, just a big stick and a bass drum and plenty
of franks and fireworks but
                        we know
              better, though
we can't say quite what we know it
to be, we stay foreign to ourselves,
so it's less barndance than
                        dervish, the step spinning away
              with a force born
of the founding furies
but pushing
                        out and on, the land's own
              dark energy feeding it,
fiddling it, and it circles,
never still, too much to believe in or feel part of but
then

we're taken by the hand and we're in it, uncertain
about the footing but bound
to it, dizzy
                        with it, caught up
              by the who-knows-where

of our whirling

here.

Plymouth Rock Dervish

Those inclined to granite and grandeur
had best try the Forefathers Monument,
Allerton Street,
                    two hundred sixteen times
            life-size, or drive
north to Duxbury, climb the Standish
tower's spiral stair
                    and there command
            a view so vast the past
can't help but feel lofty, fixed, impregnable—

because here
you're more apt to feel pity,
to think of
                    Standish's wife dead
            that first winter like
so many others,
buried at night and in secret lest
the headstones broadcast
their vulnerability,

and pity, too, for the stone itself, pissed-on
for pranks, sundered once and re-cemented,
pity for its monumental understatement,
its being just as much
                    left-behind stepping-stone
            as landing place or foundation,
launching us
                    away from each other
            toward whatever we'd make
of our freedoms,
and as Governor Bradford saw the exodus
happen, *Anno Domini* 1632, his soul
wept:

For now
as their stocks increased and the increase
vendible, there was
no longer any
                    holding them together, but now
            they must of necessity go
to their great lots,
including acres of parking lot now
where the tourists drift toward their cars

swinging their bags of vendibles:
                    miniature Mayflowers,
            scrolls of knock-off proclamations,
disposable cameras;
with a glance out through masts
and rigging at the ocean and a thought
of the
                    distances
            crossed
to come here,
then another crossed, west, ending
in ocean again;

and with that thought perhaps a last glance back
to this boulder, out of sight now
but sunk in the mind,
in the sand, in its sea of wished-upon

pennies.

Thomas Morton of Merrymount, His Dervish

...as if this jollity would have lasted ever.
—WILLIAM BRADSHAW, *Of Plymouth Plantation*

For every sure foot
that finds stone, one steps
            in the river; for
        every founder, framer, redeemer,
forgiver,

a Thomas Morton,
            the Devil's disclaimer
        to our charters and compacts and
sermons—a vermin, a Bacchus

who's turned his back on the blockhouse
            for the fringe of the polis,
        unpoliced,
with his maypole and punchbowl
and lascivious verse,

his cohorts and their Indian consorts,
barbarians, pettifoggers,
            atheists, slaves and servants
        and just plain fools all
on equal footing, not a lord
among them
save

that Lord of Misrule, Morton, who leads
them
            so merry a dance
        their spinning seems

a whirlpool into which the fragile ship
of state will surely be drawn

unless the state come
          for him first, first
      with writs demanding
he cease and desist, then to seize him
           with sword and piece
      drawn in case
he resist or be emboldened
           with ale and with
      such airy visions of
what might be

as are *contra bonos mores* and best
barred from these shores,
           or confined
     to his
poetry.

Dervish for Mike Fink, Alligator-Horse

Beeswax the children's ears and sequester your females,
and in the interests of the general peace clear
the banks of powdered French dandies and those
partial to steam travel,
                    for here he comes now, king
            of the keelboaters, round a bend
in the *belle rivière*, half
                    rattlesnake, half grizzlybear, one pole-end
        in mud and one poking the air, self-appointed
lifetime Mayor of the American Middle of Nowhere,
Mike Fink,

            crackshot hothead begat
        by a whirlwind upon floodwaters,
one-hundred percent pure alligator-horse, who ate
John Bull whole, washed him down with Kentucky whiskey,
passed him out behind
and cleaned with Federalist Papers—

you run against him, sir, you've run
            into a snag.
        No farm, no woman, no wig-pated legislature
hogties him, with his
fists big as pumpkins, a face like raincarved stone
and a brain
            that's deferred to his brawn for so long
        it's shrunk some from neglect.

Go platt your land, put down your roots, put up
your cities on the hill, he knows
            it all spills
        back down to the river, down
to him, floating his mixed load of pork, tobacco, limes,
apples, flour, beef and brooms to the Mississippi
and slipping on down
                to the German Coast and the French

plantations and New Orleans,
then a thousand miles back home by foot and horse
on the Natchez Trace just to do it again

though he knows he's cooking his own goose
helping them settle this river
and he'll have to look one day for another,
                   which won't last forever, either,
          and he'll have to come back
in new garb, as a gumshoe or gun
slinger or superhero or drop-dead rock singer,
but that's later;
                   go bung your barrels well, he'll
          whiff out whiskey fifty miles upwind
with a headcold, and go piddle
with your paddlewheelers, let the stacks belch
their puny plumes
like the feathers in ladies' hats,

he'll still
                   be whirling his jigdance to banjo
          and fiddle on a flatboat cabin roof,
sailing on while you're
settling into
                   your cities and suburbs, behind
          evergreen hedges and blockwatches,
watching your TV cowboys
and bootleggers
and vagabond martial artists and maverick
cops—
                   he'll outcuss, outdrink, outrun
          and outscrew every last one

and leave Homeland Security wondering what's
                   to be done
          with a fellow like that, with
a people like us

so lately come in from the wilderness.

Dervish for Annie Oakley

Who knew, plugging
        rabbits and squirrels back
    in Greenville,
she was punching her own
ticket out,

or that *out* would mean *here*,
Bill Cody's tanbark stage
where
        the country's surge west
    was tamed
to a few hours on a fairground,

a stand-in Custer slaughtered over and over,
town to town, by real Sioux,
and she,
        Sitting Bull's adopted
    daughter, Little Sure Shot
with her .22 plugging
tossed coins now or snuffing candleflames
or nipping the cigarette from
the fingertips of Crown Prince Wilhelm
in his pre-*Platz-an-der-Sonne* days?

Who knew the dead past would be home
to her
        dead eye, a home that's
    a roaming nowhere,
state to state to Queen Victoria's jubilee to

Edison's in West Orange where he captures
her
        on Kinetograph,
    until

her real home is a foreign distance she
crosses when she can, where
                    she sits
            with Frank one
evening and looks out on her changes
of costume flying

from the clothesline, as colorful
and strange as
the flags
                    of countries she's been to
            where people gape as
the American spectacle whirls
before them like a lariat

and the girl from Ohio shoots money
                    out of
mid-air.

Steel-Drivin' Dervish

All day long in the night-dark tunnel
John's shaker sings songs from his knees,
songs about
                    mountains with summits called
        Freedom or Rest or
Glory, Eternity, Hope, songs that climb
whole other ranges and peaks
than these Appalachians

while he steadies the spike for the whistle and ring
of John's hammer strike,
a swing
with a rock-cleaving rage
                    that feeds on those songs,
        those slopes, not one of them
being the mountain
they're dead-center of now,
where there's no glory, no summit,
but only this

gouge and blast, this eating-away at its insides
in rhythm
like a rot, a disease

that bleeds men, breeds the steel-child,
and the steam machine—and not just
the locomotive, but there's wind, too,
                    of one that will do John's job
        faster and without song
altogether.

He is himself
the stuff of song, of memory, already;
a baby-boy verse,
a twenty-pound hammer verse, a verse the Captain

likes best on how it takes just
                    three turns of John's shovel
            to make a fresh grave,

but the shaker goes on with his mountain songs,
he fires John's fury, he keeps the going
steady that way,
he beckons
                    the future, furthers and hurries it,
            brings on the end
that way, and John pounds it out in time,

knowing the end will come for him long
before any train clatters through
this hole snorting steam,
long before this tunnel is
                    lit at two ends by the daylight
            he barely gets a chance
to see,
before this country is gone wherever it's going
at such speeds, no climb,
no rest, just engine blast, *toot-sweeet, toot-sweeet,*
and wheel thunder

sounding
                    long after this one hammer's
            laid down, its whistle and ring
finished, a few verses of song,
a fresh grave.

Tombstone Dervish

They call this "The Town Too Tough to Die,"
but with its ghoulish historama
narrated by
                Vincent Price the message is
      mixed—
mixed
with the ghosts of the Spanish *presidio*,
the Apache, the prospectors,

all tough and all dead, though
here comes
               Doc Holliday riding
      his two-horse tourist wagon
down Allen Street, coughing up the bloody
past through a headset microphone.

Even the name is a soldier's joke
just good enough to stick—"All you'll find
out there is yer tombstone"—and the chuckle
            runs from that first silver strike
      through boom and bust and finally
on to this hawker's paradise,
where the deepest seam runs six feet
under:

the claims staked now aren't to silver
but to lead, street placards
marking
           the spot where someone
      too flush with that precious ore
cashed in.

A corner shop offers O K Ice Cream, history
chilled to a sweet mediocrity,
and maybe that hits

the mark, or comes
closer at least than the shootouts
staged bi-hourly

or the digital portrait we have taken
in sepia, the gunslinger and his moll,
the clothes they give us
                    only backless facades,
          the rifle's lever action twist-tied.
But the backdrop, the illusion of

endless frontier:
the truest thing
we've seen since we got here.

Lindsay's Dervish

The whirling dervish, the singing dervish...make a good parallel,
if you believe that when you whirl and call on the name of God
the sky and the stars and the universe will descend to you.
             —VACHEL LINDSAY, *Letters*

I've thought hard about it, Lindsay,
but I'm still not sure what happened, what soured,
how all those miles of
                  tramping, sowing poems
            like apple seeds
in high schools, churches, English Departments,
theaters, convents, halls,
how someone who knew the "weltering grand panorama"
of this country better than anyone,
from the bottom of your beggar's shoes to the top
of your booming voice,
and who believed beyond words in its beauty,

how someone like that comes to an end like yours—unless
that was just it,
                  the vast tours turned into an industry,
            the poetry factory cranking out
"standardized little Vachels every day like Ford cars—
a new well-varnished, guaranteed, noisy, cast-iron
Little Vachel
in every town for a year and a half, like a whirlwind,"
until it finally took you down;

or maybe the labels did that, your performances pegged
                  as "the higher vaudeville"
            or "jazz," those tags you hated most because
you knew you'd brought them on yourself
with your whooping and stomping, your crying out,

verse-dervish of these United States, starving
for real attention but "banished
like Dante and heckled by strangers" instead, "the prisoner
of a stunt."

Or maybe it was the dread of age, desperate
on the brink of 50 for "a new disorganized boyhood,"
and your prescient letters
home to Elizabeth about men at that stage who would
            "drink poison to have the general
        neatness of mind" they'd had
two decades before. "Dear heart—if there is any youth
in me enjoy it. If there is any old age for God's sake
kick it out of your bed forevermore.
You should not sleep
            with a mummy and I will protect you
        like a palace guard while you choose
a fit lover for all the rich young fruit in you."

Or did the vision simply topple of its own top-heavy weight,
the solid ground you hoofed over, the people,
the places, all turned by the poems into hieroglyphs,
John Chapman's woods become
            a fairyland, every rock an altar-stone,
        the apple farms hoisted aloft,
gospelized, sent to heaven with General Booth,
Springfield not an Illinois town but some Mecca, Mystic
Springfield, Swedenborgian Springfield,
always
            the extravagant leap beyond the thing
        itself to the thing sermonized,
the preacher's teachings, even your drawings do it,
their ostensible subjects—Lincoln's Tomb, the Presbyterian
Church—half obscured,
all but blotted out by those huge,
heaven-swung censers like the chairs of a celestial
carnival ride, the world gone hazy in the holy smoke,

an America
                etherealized clean out of its solid
       and soiled skin
until we have "Orpheus fiddlers" in "fairy Tennessee"
and a merry-go-round with "Pegasus ponies"—
Lindsay!

"Say, is my prophecy too fair and far?"
Both, I suppose—always the *mens sana*
in a sanitized body,
the "clean laws," the "clean prairie lands,"
the States "free and clean,"
and even
               the poison a cleanser,
     Lindsay,

I've thought hard about it
and still can't say what drove you to it at last, but I know
what you tried, know what you found
             to love here, how you sang
     that love out loud
in the big poems you said we needed;

and we do, still,
and you live in whoever tries writing them,
in whoever tries to call down the sky
and the stars, however unlikely, and whatever it comes to.

Ohio's 200th Birthday Dervish

Eyes closed, one wish, now open
                 and *whoosh*, out go the candles,
     snuffed
like a Youngstown blast furnace

and you're two centuries old, a long way
from your *imperio in imperium* days, no?,
your Firelands and Indian wars,

and though Syracuse, Athens, and Euclid still dot
the map
              you outgrew your classical youth,
       your ill-fitting empire suit,
or tried to, the whole country did,
more mother of exiles than brazen giant,

so no, no empire, and especially not here
in this neck of the republic, not with counties
and rivers called Wyandot, Miami,
Muskingham, Mohican, not where
             your own name is native,
      "beautiful river," three-quarter
vowel and a consonant as close as a letter
can come to silence,

no not where the ghost of John Chapman wanders
the Seven Ranges lugging his seeds
             and his Swedenborg and
      his saucepan hat, no,

though you tried, you aspired, count
your Presidents,
            but they came home shot
      or ashamed or forgotten,
not emperors, no, so the old motto went down

the river and the new one, penned
by a Dayton twelve-year-old when you
were a hundred a fifty, says,
            "With God, all things are
        possible,"
which falls about as short as "Here triumphed
in death ninety [sic] Christian Indians"
on the obelisk at Gnadenhutten
            where settlers executed
        ninety-six (thirty-nine children)
two at a time by crushing their heads
with corn mallets, yes

with God even that was possible,
yes even a river could catch fire—but let's let
that lie,
            the note's too sour, too
        easy, it's your birthday,
we're not here to toss buckeyes, we're
here to sing

and if the song falters a bit, well
then alright, it's okay
for a state
            that's not East and not West,
        both land- and waterbound, both
hillocked and plained, poisoned and pristine,
poet-stuff and pig iron and God
knows what other this/that beyond reconcile

but in any case
            two hundred, and we're
        dancing, tooting your horn,
filling your dirigible, and if it's a little bit
messy, if we get some on us,
it only means

the glass is overfull.

Fourth Dervish

My! People come and go so quickly here!
                    —DOROTHY

If we'd been twistered
            away to some wizard-land, this
        spewing of fire and smoke smack
in the street's middle would mean a witch
were arriving (or departing)—a Bad one, too,
since the Good sort come
and go silently in dish-soap bubbles,
even their speech
squeaky clean—

but, no:
though it's neither home nor Kansas, we know
right where we're at and when the show
fizzles there's only children
whooping, adult applause, the humid dark,
only this collection of friends
            and strangers, philosophers,
        brokers, teachers, anthropologists,
occupational therapists, kayakers, musicians,
in a suburb of Franklin's Philadelphia,

to which he himself returned
            rarely in the end, Venerable Master
        of the Lodge of *Les Neuf Soeurs*,
not even
when his own wife died,
and from which his illegitimate son
            withdrew forever—to England,
        the final insult.

Our host is my cousin—who shares his birthday
with the nation's, whose siblings are not here
            but in Phoenix, Seattle, Carbondale,
      Atlanta, Portland—
and his wife, from Bangladesh, whose headaches
have returned since her Chinese
acupuncturist vanished, the phone
            disconnected. Their marriage is not
      her first—there is, in fact, not one
mutual first marriage here; we've all of us lived
            elsewhere,
      loved others.
Some of these children are the proof.

Tomorrow we'll affirm again our independence,
            disperse to our take-offs
      and turnpikes, our own streets
and trees and water pressures and coffee brands,
our particular bedcreaks and bugbears,
but for now there's that other claim,
binding
and unspoken, the one that raises
these glasses, that brings us here to this house
on this day,

this day we half
            despise for its inebriate
      flag waving, its gratuitous
rockets and bombs, but which
today has something of the right feel to it,
something that flares up
in the chest and lets us warm to this
slightly delirious spectacle,

which a month later when we think back
will seem like some whirling dance or
            a dream delighted in and then,
      woken from, doubted,

as such bonds and allegiances are bound to be
here,
where we hardly can say what holds us together
or what shared place it is
that we come from, and since no account
or photograph or keepsake
                   can balloon us back to it.
          But no need, really,
since you, and you, and you
were all there.

II
Our Ships

Tour Guide, Fallingwater

This could be the radio, droning
A snow-day's closings and postponements.
Each word is a sandstone
Slab in a wall, a grey permanence,

Transitions as matter-of-course
As the route from room to room
Back home, rote corridors.

Here is a knowing that's forgotten
The tongue, the cave it's housed in,

Its fluent life in the breath-stream.

But listen: *We are founded now on rock,*
Says the house, *and now on thin air.*
Be both at home, when you get back,
And bewildered at belonging there.

When She Was Gone

O, house, were we not good? When did lack
Not send its haloes of whole notes through the
roof?
Indie, weren't we, my sour little grudge-band?
Red brick and baking stone, did we not rock,
Were we not simply the limit, the end,
With our spine-piercing riffs in the trouble clef?

Testing, I said into a mic wired with gin.
*Testing, one, one, one. If my best foot
Be in the room, would it make itself known?*
It wouldn't. Nor would the *forward* to put it.
O, house, what wheels did we not spin?
What backups and gushings, no, downspout?

I'd start lines with *She was…*, just to see how far
Short of the mark they'd fall. I'd cry foul,
Then for free-throw heave my pentameter air-ball.
Build what I would, it all came to furniture—
Not a house, was it, house? Not a room, rooms.
An imagined grandeur stalled at columns.

I went into you, then—your lath and plaster, your
Every-which-ways of wire and soldered copper.
Into your fires and waters, threads and sparks,
To see how the heart of just one thing works.
But nothing I learned would have stopped her.
O, house: the heart is your open and terrible door.

The Death of Orpheus

(the bacchantes)

So there was Mr. Music with his one
Big grief. On and on and on.
Only a cypress or two still listened. One stone.

"Going Out of My Head." "I Fall to Pieces."
Just lame covers, now. No new releases.
It was as if Eurydice's

Second death
Killed anything he had left inside to work with.
He was a strained soup: no solids, just broth.

And the lyre. It used to be he'd coax
God's own orchestra out of that thing, the *vox
Divina*. Now it was all about the ex-

And who *wouldn't* have turned around, etc.
We thought: better a
Mournful silence, a mute grief; get her a

Nice headstone, a scholarship or tuition waver
Named after her. Whatever—
But get over

It. Instead, he went on picking those heart-
Strings like a scab, each new arpeggio of hurt
Ripping him further apart.

They say his neglect drove us to insanity,
Like he was god's gift to women, to humanity!
In a way, he was. But the rest's a lie—in reality,

We'd plead his case to each other: *Remember,*
We'd say, *he's been to hell and back for her.*
The truth of it was, he was still there.

He didn't need us to tear him to pieces.
When he died, the animals closed on Thrace's
Bard; and where the notes had been—those noises.

Orpheus in America

His power chords would rock the forest.
The trees and stones gathered round,
Made a blockhouse, a fort, a stage.

He descended to hell with his song,
With the electric twelve-string, just to see
What would happen. He wowed them.
The hell-hound slobbered with admiration.

Behind every successful man, he said,
There's a woman. He turned around
To be sure, and she went up like kindling.

The world lay all before him. He could park
Anywhere. But none of the animals came
Anymore.

He fingered dirge after dirge. He wailed.
Drunk women paraded past, raised their skirts
And said, *Well?*

He'd sworn off their love. They tied him
To a fence post and tore that faggot up.

Parts of him still wash ashore on the banks
Of poisoned rivers—a hand with eight fingers,
A huge red ear like half a valentine.
They get thrown back. Small fish.

That's his mother, Calliope, in the Radio
Shack, selling headphones. Pregnant—
Always pregnant, by some god.

The Dish and the Spoon Come Home

If that little dog laughs one
More time, they'd both said.
Add to that the cat's scratchy
Fiddle, a cow on the wrong medication,
A night lit for travel.

At first the sheer cheek
And the fairytale, these
Were enough. They pictured
The gapes like an oven door dropped open.

But soon the dish was remembering
Mates, all their old jokes
About flatware. How they would titter
In stacks when the fridge motor ran.
And the spoon thought of bowls,
The lips and flanks of bowls.
The dish was so slight,
No more than a saucer, in fact.

The dish said *Look at my blue*
Border of vines. The spoon said
In a pickle I could dig my way out.
The dish spun circles, humming.
The spoon got under a lid and pried.

It was no good. The spoon met
Another spoon and they joined
A band. The dish drifted over
The tablecloth, a moon with no planet.

One night the dog's nose lifted:
They're coming, he said.
The cat stopped, held the bow

As if it were a teacher's pointer
And the next lesson were stars.
The cow came down.
They're coming back.

The first nights were awkward.
Once, they both wound up
On the counter, used and dirtied,
The spoon resting smack
In the dish's middle, the handle
Stuck over the edge like a gangplank.

But the dog, to its credit,
Gave it a rest. Even the cow
Made do a few nights with the two
Moons in the cat's eyes.
And the black cat
Dreamt of good luck and perfect pitch,
Of solos so lovely the galleries
Of china and silver were solaced.

Hunger

(on reading how three Mexican fisherman survived, lost at sea nine months)

> *Was he an animal, that music could move him so? He felt as*
> *if the way to the unknown nourishment he longed for were*
> *coming to light.*
>
> —KAFKA, *The Metamorphosis*

The paper tells the months, the miles
Off course. It names you and the two
Who starved, translates as "tossed"
The way you put them overboard. It calls
"Storm" how the doom–ship's
Dark sails massed overhead.
The Pacific, we learn, is "wide."

Wide is
The blue between some hungers
And words for them. Not
Hunger hunger, the one a few lines
Of cable can tackle,
The ends barbed with bent parts
From the spent engine,
The catch you hauled in and ate raw.

And not the hunger that called less for
A *hauling-in* than a *calling-down*,
That had you kissing the Bible
Like you would dry land
If you lived through this, you said—
Even a lubber knows that one, calls
His faith a rock.

I'm thinking of the hunger you say
You fed with old ballads, rock 'n roll,
And dance. What species of famine
Feasts on song? What hunger gluts itself
On the slides and bends of air guitar,
All the knobs cranked,
The face contorted halfway between
Birthpain and rapture?

Wide is any sky you get so lost beneath
Your fingers suddenly fly
On the fret board, high up on the neck
Of nothing, eyes wincing back
At spotlights of sea glare,
Way out there and wailing.

A Translation Lexicon

The key term is *volatile*,
Not only for its etymological
Link to wings and flight, though that's essential;

And not just for its host of apt associations,
Such as changeability, potential for violence,
Explosiveness, instability, impermanence,

The capacity to turn all at once into vapor,
Liveliness—in short, the anti-torpor
That marks any act of translation proper;

But for this: with the dictionary open to *volatile*,
The whole rest of the lexicon is available
On those two pages alone. For example:

Voltage,
That electricity born when language
Meets language and writer writer—that wattage.

And *vivify*,
To impart vitality, to give
Language its second life.

Of course, *vocabulary* and *voice*.
Vocation, which means, despite thinking twice,
Going on like there's really no choice.

On one crucial term, here, current theory says little.
In fact, nothing. *Vodka*. Though its role is subtle,
To leave it out altogether is fatal:

When the voltage is low,
The language wingless; when there's no way, no how,
And you find yourself brow to brow

With the *void* (another key
Term); *vodka* switches on the electricity,
Gets you thinking *this thing might fly*

After all, and what before seemed a dead-end appears
An opportunity, now. Still others
Name work gone awry: *volte-face* refers

To that about-face you do ten
Stanzas into it, when to go on would be a sin,
So you turn back and start again.

Then there's *vivisection*, which means
Hacking something into translated smithereens
And losing all sense

Of the living whole. Also relevant
Is the other *void*, the verb, for when what was meant
As translation comes out as excrement.

And so that this lexicon may further re-animate
The discipline, let us not forget
It includes the word for when things come right—

For the feeling that will follow,
And which no misgivings will belie:
Voilà.

The First Translation

Back then, the ear was a tool, like a trowel;
Little more than a hand for grabbing sound.
Not an orchid, yet; no roots in the soul—
That needed gods to scatter and confound

Us, and strangers to come and speak some cross
Between a clogged pipe and an orgasm.
What it named left us at a total loss.
Here: sound. There: thing. In between, a chasm

Where the meanings had been pitched like old tires.
We stood there staring from the sink-hole's brink,
Our tongues stunned by the jumble of crossed wires.
That's when the parched ear reached down for new drink

At last, with a root that by-passed the think-tank,
Vining down the vocal chords, till it touched
The sea from which our lives first crawl, and sank
Deep in. The water climbed and when it reached

The ear, the ear flowered outward toward all
It hadn't fathomed yet—not just the speech
Of strangers, but the suddenly orchestral
Music of what we'd thought familiar, each

Object and live thing like an instrument
Only now invented, only now played.
Once, we'd have shrunk back, unsure what it meant;
Now we'd grown patient of meaning and stayed

Simply to listen, no more bewildered
Than a blossom is, bathed in light. The ear,
Fed with first waters, basked in what it heard,
In sound singing itself, utterly clear.

And so when the strangers returned and spoke,
When the same valley opened up between
Sound and sense, rather than stand there dumbstruck
We clambered down to hear what we might glean

From the place. First, the air spoke its new name;
Then stone, river, sun; and soon, a welter
Of words, enough to build with. But this time,
No trowel, no tower—instead, a shelter

Of shared sounds reared by the ear in blossom.
And under that canopy we sat down
In silent delight, scanning the chasm—
Golden in late light, a vast seam of nouns.

Forward My Mail to the Villa, or Not

Morning, like a lost scroll found. But it rolls out
To be just one of those tourist posters of doors—
As if I needed reminding how being shut
Can fill an address book and a wheel of colors.

I'm the man who paints windows on his wall,
Where nowhere's lemon, mid-morning eternity
Lifts the eye over tile roofs and trees down to a bay
That harbors waves of suspicion and ill will;

The man who will rise for the anthem of an echo,
For a seed from the dried fruit of a bargain book.
That a thing can flourish by being pinched back,
That's my zen. That's a diet I can stick to.

I'm told there's a war on. And that Time persists
As the dust-factory's grandfatherly, kind CEO.
Rachel, the hurricane, bears down. Let her blow:
In my window pointillist trees shake like fists.

Bad Magic

This hour and the next will try to pull
Me out of myself, scarf after
Scarf, a trick called The Human Shell,
Performed to canned laughter.

When all I want is to live
Without that bad magic, without a gear
That turns the wheel that saws me in half,
Or an ad that makes me disappear—

Without the light breaking in like a fist
That slowly (*drum roll!*) unfolds
Once I've guessed
What path, what possibility it holds,

Only to show me what I'd hoped for
Is held in another hand.
I only want each hour hinged like a door,
An invitation, a new route, the ampersand

That fends off the full-stop's standstill;
A light like a chord that rings
The bell of itself, that trumpets its arrival,
Spills its ballast of offerings.

It's no easy thing, since the world
Expects to peer into its upturned top hat
And, *voilà*, find you there, curled,
The thimble-rig's dependable rabbit.

I want that hat to go *poof* in self-fire;
The brutal centrifuge of the second hand
To go haywire
Until it dangles, defunct. A broken wand.

Proposing to the Widow DeWine

1.5 seedy little acres. Ranch. 2 bedrooms.
Carport. Hardly more than a cardboard box
To someone like DeWine. But it served.
He'd stocked it with toys—
Hot tub, big screen, bar. Tossed a duplicate
Key on my desk once, big tip for the years
Of sound counsel. That wink of his, too
Slow, those watery eyes. Picture time-lapse
Footage of a bad gash closing over. The key
Landed clean in one day's square on my desk
Calendar and I thought of hopscotch and that
Made it worse, somehow. Once he bought me
The 45 of "Mr. Lonely." I could call him
Mr. Networth. We got on well enough.

This was the first she'd heard of it, the will.
And she knew. Right off. And wanted to drive
By—to see it, to torch it, to hurt more,
To hate more, who knows—and handed me her keys.
It all felt so bad I couldn't look at her eyes.
Her mouth turned a thin line, a bare branch
Where there'd been cardinals. I had my first
Two afternoon appointments scratched.

You had to go under the freeway, out past
The last motels, their hyphenated husband-wife
Names, their big pitch still TV and AC, past
The roadhouse and its busted EATS arrow aimed
Straight for the ground. But when the turn came
She was still going, how one night nearly asleep
She thought she smelled him, how he was two
Days dead when the bookstore called to say his *Guide
To Longer Living* by Fredericks was in, and she
Almost pulled something trying not to laugh.

And so I kept going, too, on into the townships
Of the plastic deer, the water pump, the cupped
Mesh petals of the satellite dish, its black
Stamen coaxing signal down in swarms. Soon
The hottest things going were pancake breakfasts
And clean fill. Townships where the neighbor's
Light was a distant star, where you could drop
Dead and feed the whole household of starving cats
For a week before anyone looked in. Townships
Of steeples and silos, cars on blocks, dogs,
Even, with one bad wheel, tops of drives turned
Attics, piled with tires, water heaters, odd
Lumber, siding, busted pipe, bucket seats,
Put to some last piecemeal use like organ donors.

We'd kept quiet a while. The *shhh* of the tires.
To the window she said your yard was just
Wherever you stopped mowing out here.
I looked over, at the light catching one silver
Hair like a river seen from a plane, at
The ivory beads of her earrings like bedsheets
Knotted and dropped from a window. Now the grass
Outside grew high as a dashboard, then the ground,
Turned up and combed out to the treeline,
A blackbird flying stunts over the rows, over
The old grain places, and before I could think
Better of it or think of all the good reasons
In the world to say no my own words flew the space
Between us, over the seat, as if they too obeyed
An instinct for some vital, half-remembered thing,
And meeting silence looped and dove and rode
The thermals keeping the glass clear and us warm.
Until they grew so strange and finally irksome
They might as well have been birds, slapping
At the windows, the moon roof, frantic for
Real sky and gliding room, scratching the bad
Bark of the upholstery.

The whole way back the road seemed to dip, my
Stomach was doing that. Like falling. Only up.
It registered—our passing the turn again, out
My side this time—but only later, in the office,
After she'd gone. I was staring through blinds,
Wondering which of those good reasons were hers,
And what mine were for asking; for anything;
And if those weren't my words there, wheeling
Through the new federal building's girder frame,
Set free at last through the open, considerate
Vowel of her reply.

Bruxism

While we're asleep, the brain tends
To the animals.
It drops the electric fence
And they hurry out, they've waited all day.
They wander through town
Down the middle of streets, it's alright,
They know the benevolent mayor here
And his brother the butcher
Who sits outside the locked door
Of his shop and smokes
A joint, watching and laughing.

But while they play there's one comes out
Just to feed.
And means business.
We give it the scraps of our waking
Hours, the undigested reading,
The leftover paperwork.
All day it sits loathing our little completions,
Our balanced checkbooks, our good loving
And sent letters; and our competence,
Anyone blowing the smallest horn
Of praise for us—
It paces, drags its deaf ear around the cage.

But let us get started
On gun control, on crime, on our own
Undervalued worth, anything we can't
Resolve or conclude, and it perks up, it smacks
Its lips.
We say *capital punishment*, it
Turns on its back and wriggles against
The cement. We say *republican, democrat*,
It sits up and licks itself.

It loves our impossible children
Like its own pups. It loves how we sit there
And picture ourselves in other jobs,
With other lovers.
We check the clock, it purrs.
It goes moony over our lists of errands,
It can smell a feast of the not-done.

So later, someone beside us wakes
To our gnashing and grinding, shoves us
Halfway to the brink of consciousness,
And it steps back from the trough.
But not for long.
And it will be hours, yet, till the thin air
Of our failures fills it up

And it lopes back behind the fence
With the others and we sit at daybreak
At the bed's edge testing
The sore hinge of the jaw, trying to recall
Why Audrey Hepburn needed our help
So desperately.

The Life Dog

Throw this mutt a bone, it comes back fleshed-out.
Sure, his runt days were make-do and hind-tit,
But don't go by the bark—this is the bite

That's dragged some sure goners back from the brink.
Living's his chow, he's rabid for it—think
Lassie, but hyped on meds from the pet-shrink.

You'll see him clawing-out holes in the sod,
But the only thing he'll bury is seed.
He'll shake, roll over; but he won't play dead.

And won't stay put—his leash is the Great Chain
Of Being, and the one whistle he'll run
For, we can't hear: the soul, in mortal pain.

Then he works his magic. He laps the wound,
It closes. He runs three circles around
The fallen, they stand. His growl has summoned

The departing spirit back. And meanwhile,
His peers chase cars and squirrels, face-down the mail-
Man, turn a colorblind eye from the ill.

The life-dog wonders what it's coming to
When the goal's a good screw or Best in Show.
It's not right; this is not what best friends do.

Hans Asperger and the Bomb, 1944

Some dust never settles.
He stood in what had been his hospital's

Doorway, wondering which dust was stone, which
Wood, which paper. The only research

Was the air's particled, patient inquiry
Into absence, into the history

Of human undoing. Fires,
Explosions—he'd heard them as metaphors

For the flashing of brain signals, the mind's
Non-stop night-raids on what it can't understand;

But these were literal, and opposite.
Where he stood was no doorway but a dot

On a strategist's map
Of what had once been Europe,

A full stop ending a line
Of gibberish. Standing there, he'd already begun

Making the next sentence,
And making it make a kind of sense.

Hans Asperger at School

The most direct and advisable route
To winning his peers' esteem, it turned out,
Was *not* to recite

From memory and for its sheer pleasure
The verse of Franz Grillparzer
Or display an agitation verging on seizure

When one of them bent a rule.
No, for this he was not made to feel
A part of their circle, but like a soul

In one of Dante's.
Still, if being a soul meant doing without bodies,
That might be best: the body—his,

At least—was an awkward, unresponsive vehicle
Fashioned only to encourage ridicule.
But even for a circle

Of Hell he'd somehow be found
Unfit. His was the endless, useless round
Of his own involute mind.

He supposed there was no one like him in all
The world. He wondered was he ill.
And would he get well. And what was it called.

Snow Day

Today's word from on-high is: yellow's cancelled.
Sun. Parking lot lines. School bus and lead pencil.
It's compound weather: white-out, homebound, standstill,

Shutdown. What to do with nowhere to go,
Mind? The wind suggests *chill*. *Drift*, says the snow.
By degrees, you'll find that you sink below

Your level head's all-wheel drive to remain
On top of things. You'll go tunneling, brain,
Past your own bedrock and last bottom line

To the white space preceding every poem,
And following, too. To the blizzard room,
The brain storms of conception, the come-from

And did-that of the mind in self-delight
At what its weather might precipitate—
And has. The blank slate's polar opposite.

No need to give in, dig out. Stay, unhurried,
In the snow fort, angel-making and flurried-
On till that last yellow, *Caution*, lies buried

And all roads to and from are pure invention.
Look: your breath is the exhaust of an engine
Revving; your mind's a blade, the fast ice inch-thin.

His Preference for Winter

Summers, the South Avenue bars
From the Classique to The Coconut
Grove leave their doors thrown

Open, and the car windows are down,
The house windows up, and everyone's
Business billows
Out, a jukebox of curses, cries,
The hustle and stab of the voices.

And the skin, too, is outloud, exposed.
Slick and sexhungry
On the young; on the old,
Slack and stained by illness,
A threadbare bonesack.

So even while he trades
With a neighbor the usual gripes about
The grips of winter—the stiff joints,
Shoveling, gas bills—secretly
He loves its shutdown and shelter,
Its muffled music,

And the way snow tones
The city back to a black and white
Photograph, plain shades of sky
And millstack, silent and severe
The way time is or duty or death.

He can almost hear the pilot
Lights flutter.
The bar doors stay shut and the skin
Under wraps. When he sees
The smoking rooftops he thinks

Of a town in an old war,
Besieged, emptied, the flesh having
Fled before some large
And mighty force whose advance
Is relentless, steady, cold.

Cold

People are dying—which is no big secret.
But of course it's *the* big secret; only now,
Late February, it's getting harder to keep,
With the wind not giving
A damn like this and the months of cold
Having finally found out where we live, here
Under the skin.

The sheer accumulated mass
Of bitching starts to weigh on rooftops
Everywhere—about black ice, pot-holes,
About being duped by that one coatless
Day. But really it's about the fact that
That bare, ungainly tree out front,
The one they've lopped to make
Way for the power lines, will still be there
After we're dead. That piece of shit tree.

It's on the tips of our tongues, it's written
In the mist we're breathing, those voice-balloons:
I'm not driving to Aunt Cheryl's in this stuff,
I'm dying; what's the point
Of shoveling now, with two more inches
On the way, and me dying?; these pants aren't
Worth a damn against this wind, but
I'm dying, and they'll do to be buried in.

Valentine's Day is so that we can maybe cling
To chocolate here in February
When it becomes plain that we're dying,
Which we knew already, but then
We were warm and the sky didn't seem so
Headstone-colored and we figured, hell,
No one dies in a tee-shirt like this, though we
Didn't know we were thinking that.

What we do know is that dying in February,
The way we are,
Will lack any nobility or grandeur whatever—
We'll just be cold, and it goes slower
Than traffic in a white-out, like watching
Icicles form,
The slow drip that leaves the eaves fanged.

Even if we're blown to cinders in some
Sick, local-anti-insurgency-effort daydream
And they have to ID us through dental records
So they know whom they're burying the medal
With, our teeth—lying there in the rubble
And smoke—will be those gag dentures
Chattering on, still bitching about the pipes,
The freeze, how the oil prices are killing us.

Our Ships

They're out there
Alright,

Their wakes a wedge of ocean
Fat as our slice of the pie, deep
As the dark hold where all we've got
Coming, and then some, rides.

O they're handsome, they're fine,
Prow to poop deck, keel
To crow's nest.
The sun turns cleats, pulleys, trim
To doubloons. Our names
Are stenciled on the hull in a blue
Straight out of our future's clear sailing.

But where? And *when*? It's not that
They're lost, misled, the captain
With patches on both eyes,
His map scrolled and bow tied on the shelf
By his sheepskin from the dunce academy,

No—nor that the deckhands
Are all thumbs; they run the rigging
As if their own bodies had spun the stuff.
Anchors, mermaids, Neptunes
Bob on their busy arms.

No, they're out there, our ships.
Their sails belly
Like our grandfathers' shirtfronts
Who stepped off the boat
Into their bootstrap-and-slave-wage sagas
Of success.

But it may be at heart
They're discoverers, they're in love
With the passage, not the port,
And they're out to enlist the like-hearted
On land by the distance they keep,
Which brings us down to the shoreline
Imagining, scanning horizon
Through the spyglass of our rolled-up
Times, tribunes, sentinels.
Until

One day, having pictured
So hard, imagined so deeply, we go
Wobbly, we're all at sea, we're attending
To breeze, sand, scent,
To our own beautiful earth-made mass,
The lubber's first love;

And what comes into view
Is finally something like land, something
Like the new world all over, right under
Our feet. So
We go, printing the stones
With our wet shoes, down our Spanish-
Named streets, to the banks
Of our *belles rivières*, Cuyahogas,
Maumees,

To futures not so different from daybreaks,
White at the window, a ship's sail
In the offing.

III
If You Lived Here

Snap the Whip

Centrifugal, those first places: circles
Widening away from the house, the yard—
The limits you were supposed to have feared
Left behind in the dust wake of bike wheels.

Your father swings you flat out around him,
Then slows till you touch down in a leaf pile.
At school it's planets, orbits, tether ball,
Apollo's round-the-moon slingshot for home.

Your big brother spins the ride in the park
So fast the world blurs, unless you can reach
The slow center; the perimeters teach
More dizzy physics than you can stomach.

And it's there at the heart of *snap the whip*,
Too, this same first law of circles, centers,
Flyaway force, one of whose articles
States that you shall be made to lose your grip

On the hands of those running beside you—
Those who, in their turn, hold another's hand,
A charging nine-member line—when one end
Pulls up, digs in, becomes the centrifuge

From which a surge, like laughter, emanates,
Ripples down through the line of hands, and *snap*,
It arrives at the end, at the whip's tip.
The last two are the first it separates,

And they go headlong for the summer grass;
Then the next two, as the line circles round
This new hub; then everyone's on the ground,
Content to be gravity's thralls at last.

And you don't notice the white train of cloud
About to be drawn across the sun's face,
Or the cap, ten yards off, like the last trace
Of someone who's simply stepped below ground,

Or even the black slab of open door
In the distance, over near the grownups—
None of the small signs telling you you'll glimpse
This moment again, years and miles from here,

When what you've tried to hold has slipped your grip
And you're stretched out in park grass, not quite sure
How the force arrived: but less like *laughter*
This time. More than ever like *lash*, like *snap*.

One Hallow's E'en,

After hours, and the stock procession

Of brides, buccaneers, quarterbacks,
Ranch hands, I half expect

To answer one last knock
And find a boy with my own dark

Hair, left long in back; and his eyes,
Their kindness, their relish—yours.

No get-up, no bag; for masquerade,
The substance of a living child.

Seen from the street,
I'll seem a man who thought

His own front stoop preposterous
Or the world beyond his door an enormous

Prank: jack o' lantern grins gone
Drunken, their roofs caved in;

Neighbors' old sheets haunting
Oaks and maples; leaves blown chattering

Against curbs, or still on their
Limbs shivering like sheet after

Sheet of not quite the right words crumpled.
And if I'm seen to reach for empty

Air, to hold it close, they'll say I've
Been too long beneath that halved

Apple of a moon, its lonely watch
Passing nearly close enough to touch.

Tent

It was the first time
I'd really seen rain, seen it
Come on, advance like that—
Across a lake in Maine, the water
Behind it scuffed and dulled, the air
Smudging like a charcoal sketch.
We barely beat
The storm back to the tent,
My brother and I, my father.
Inside, while the wind ho-hummed
And the rain drummed fingers
On the canvas, Dad
Did card tricks, monkeyed
With the radio reception, told
Some racy jokes I pretended hard
To get. Beyond the mesh
Of the zippered door the canoe
Lay beached and flipped, its red
Belly etched silver
As the chub that tugged
Our lines all day.

Now, the two boys are mine,
And "tent" the eldest's favorite
Game: he and his brother,
His mother and I, packed together
On the floor in the front room
Holding a crib blanket
Above our heads. No rain—
Shipwreck waves of sunshine
Busting in through three windows;
And floating the channels of light,
Swirling into view
And out again, schools of dust.

Huddled there, the blanket much
Too small for all
Of us, I'm staring out
Like it's the first time
I've seen dust—really seen it,
Coming on.

American Legend

Crude wounds that meant love:
They've made a scroll
Of this tree trunk, scored it
With paired initials. Some
Filling hearts. Some with *plus* signs,
The simple math the future
Can feel like. And they mean
Love still, whatever's become
Of the people these names
Belong to.

My sons scavenge the creek bed
Below for fossils, bones, signs:
In every sharp stone an arrowhead,
Each mass of mossed rock a design.

The eldest brings me a branch
Scored across at intervals so regular
He concludes it's an artifact—his hunch
Is a calendar,

And he conjures up a feral child
Who made a haven of these thickets
And ledges, the American wild,
Marking suns on a stick.

Of my life with his
And his brother's mother
There's little trace beyond the letters
Of our last name. And the boys themselves.
And then one quarter-moon
Carved in the wood
Of her tabletop

Where I slammed down a kettle—
The gong of struck metal
A key to which every other strain
In that house might tune;

Or a bang
So big the universe might spring
From that moment re-created.
But it produced only
That moon, eaten and lonely,
Its veneer of sky unconstellated.

As for *BC* and *TS*, carved in this tree,
Sharing their arrow-pierced heart—
Now three hundred pages keep them apart
In the city directory;
Their child, perhaps, split
Them like a weed splits a stone,
Then out
Of an instinct for origins
Ran off, sheltered here one
Quarter-moon night,
Then another, kept track
On the stick my son's found.

Let's say he's returned long since
To the world, but with enough
Of this place in his blood
That he stands at a window watching
His own children chalk forests,
Lemon suns, dinosaurs,
Onto the drive, and is
Bewildered.

As I am now.
The youngest comes up the hill
With a stone, to say how
Its every nick and scratch
Holds a story he's breathless to tell—
And which,

Before he even
Speaks, I believe.

Ben's Scripts

So much of trying to raise him
Has been feeding him
Lines that come more or less naturally
To the rest of us—
And feeding him the pills that would help,
We thought, to make those lines come
More or less naturally—

That I'm astonished now, after all
This time, to find that the word for those
Illegible scrawls, those tickets
Admitting one to the world's fair
Of social skills, is *scrip*, not *script*.

Even his own speech comes out
As rehearsal. "God," he says
From the back seat, "our idea of sci-fi
Sure is different from the past." Then,
Four seconds later: "God,
Our idea of sci-fi in the present sure is
Different from what it was in the past."
Then maybe twice more, changing tones,
The last meant to be his version
Of casual, a little laugh thrown in after
The "God."

Scripts. I've been writing his lines year
After year, and he remains the master
Ad libber. God, his idea of what's
Appropriate sure is different from what
Mine is. You'd think he'd get it. Or
That I would. That he'd enter on cue
At last, in the mask I've made for him.

In a journal from five years back,
Having cleaned him up and put him
To bed, for *wash* I make this slip:
Tonight, at bedtime, I was his face
For him, and he yells.

Pedestrian

It's dwindled, of course, our going
A pied, like our attention spans
And our knowledge of wood.
And no one seems to mind this, much;
No movement is afoot to say *erect*
After we say *walk*, and thus invoke
Evolution and a respect
Bordering on awe
For our upright progress, for freeing up
The paws for other purposes.

Your best walks have always been
For love's sake—crossing whole
Cities, walks so long the flowers
Were dead when you got to her door.
And away from love, too, those
Six mid-summer miles
When the whole machine of your legs
Was greased with oils so crude
You'd never give out.
That marathon of shame and rage.

We've forgotten that the brain paces,
That the heart thumps the footfalls
Of our blood's travel.
We've outrun ourselves—was there
Ever a time when our legs were this
Disappointed?

On the floor overhead, your wife's
Step, your son's, then the other son's,
All as distinct as their voices.
You've gone stride for stride with them.
You know exactly who's coming
Down the stairs right now.
You know that body, its weight
And balance—that beautiful beast,
Hoofing it.

Seeing You

We are only lightly covered with buttoned cloth; and beneath these pavements are shells, bones and silence.
—VIRGINIA WOOLF, *The Waves*

Since we'd only just thrown clothes on
Before the first guests arrived,
I could still see you stepping back
Into the dress I love
Almost more than any *undress,*

Still hear the zipper like a far engine
Cutting out, which meant your flesh
Had been spirited away
Out of earshot for now, though moments
Before it had sung.

Now I was watching you across the yard
Talking with friends, your glass of sangria
Emptied down to the fruit,
And it was how each of our bodies
Knew the other—could depend upon, pleasure
In, the other's shape and smell,

Though distanced now
By thirty feet, thirty minutes
And buttoned cloth—
That brought it home to me, what I'd known
For days:

Next week I'll pack up my two sons,
Drive back through Reservations,
Glacier scars, from one lake
(Great) to another (Finger), and wake
To what I can hardly imagine:
My father making his way with a walker.

And when you called over the small fence
To our neighbor, eighty-five, so frail
Her own clothes
Will soon drag her down, who fell
Last week and when I'd helped her up
Said *I'm no good for shit anymore,*
And whose bones surface
More and more like the legend of some lake
Proving true—when you asked

If there was anything she'd like,
The answer in her face
Was what you might hear if you could hold
A tree to your ear like a shell:
The wind through the bare lot that was here
When she came from Hungary in forty-five,
The year my father
Went hot-shotting his Corsair
Up the Monongahela, under the bridges
At Pittsburgh, and came home

To this very town.
Back then he stood taller than this
Huge oak behind me, its two trunks
Rising from one seed.

If there's a candle to light the body's way
Through this world it's the glass
Of sliced fruit soaked red
You were holding out then, and I wanted
To go to you, to say all this just
By touching you, by taking your arm;

But the distance grew daunting,
So mixed up
With my father, with our neighbor
And the bright silver claw of her walker,
That I doubted my legs would convey me,
Or my arms convey what I meant.

Practice Elegy for My Father

This kite-flying wind, these slow-drift grays
Feathered with white, a rain that will be hours
Filling the shallow birdbath

Are all that's left of a storm that once launched
An exodus for shelter, then seized on the roofs
Of the emptied houses and peeled them back
Like the pull-tab lids of our cat food.

It made trees kiss the ground in its presence.
Rivers paid an homage so over-the-top
Our cars became their new beds' bright stones.

We threw numbers at it: severity, miles
Per hour, damage's dollar-worth, the dead,
The year of something like it. But it ate
The numbers and spat their shells back
In our faces,

Those faces on the news the next day, people
Picking through what had been their lives.

Then somewhere over Georgia or the Carolinas
It ate so many numbers it lost its appetite
For its own whirling life. It tugged and tugged
But the roofs stayed put, it could manage only
A few dead limbs. And now it drags through Ohio
Like this, barely recognizable.

The name we'd given it, like we would a child,
Is on no one's lips anymore. It's part
Of the record, a date, forgotten except by those
Few people bending in sun and an easy wind,
Lifting out a shoe, a comb, a shirt, a picture frame,

A hand-written recipe like a post card from
That new place in themselves where they'll have
To begin to go on.

Broken Crown

(Jack fell down...)

White

A kind of fall, a dream descent through white
To get here: first cloud, then snow in the mountains,
Then San Xavier's bleached dome on the right
As I drop south and find him asleep, bent

Forward in the wheelchair. The worn, white flag
Of his hair. Beneath that, a cabernet
Colored bruise. And on the left side a jagged

Scar from the first fall runs temple to scalp.
My mother's glad, she says, I could come help.

She says, *Who'd have thought we'd see him this way?*

I kiss his head—something I've never done—
As if, for what's broken there, that will do:
He'll wake and work right again, like snapped bone
When the cast comes off. Like a dream. Like new.

Time Zones

There, your new day's come. Night's dream cast have taken
Off their antlers, crowns, eyebrows; and the stage's
Grimm woods, your childhood house and haunts—all broken
Down. You record it in two notebook pages.

Here, hours later, it comes for us, too: me,
Mother, father. But the curtain won't close—
Day keeps dream's arm-length from reality,

She, spooning him fruit; he, tugging his shirt
And stuck at her name, *Roberta, Roberta,*

I, off in the word-loud glade, ten rhymed rows.

And the mountains, the sheer scale, the wide open
Skies—eternities, everywhere. It's like
Somewhere east his death has already happened,
And that day's darkness heads this way to break.

Alzheimer's

His head is a day that won't break, stays dark.
A phrase wobbles forward, teeters, and drops.
I'm falling, he cries, when we ease him back
On the bed. Then, *Am I okay?* He sleeps.

Tokens of his dementia fill the room.
Oak shelf-fuls of mail-ordered classics, hardbound,
Untouched. Plastic binders, fifty of them,

Stuffed with pages torn out of magazines.
Of the lotto tickets there are no signs—

He bet their savings, then maxed-out each card

Before she'd cottoned-on. She half-wisecracks:
I could shoot him. He'd always said don't worry,
When it came his time he'd do the Dutch act.
Now, back in his chair, to no one: *I'm sorry.*

A Many-Splendored Thing

"I'm sorry." "For what? Sit back in the chair."
He takes his shirt off. "Don't take your shirt off,"
She says; "you're looking more like your mother,
Do you know that?" "That's what I'm afraid of,"

And his laugh's a half-smile; hers is out-loud.
"I'm in agony." "I'm bathing you, what
Are you in agony for?" "Time for bed."

"No, it's *not* time for bed. You just got up.
Hold still. Agony. Don't give me that crap.

I'll give you agony in a minute."

She holds the jug under him. "I'm going.
Who's that?" They watch TV. She: "Bill Holden."
He: "In what?" "Love's a Many-Splendored Thing."
Strings soar. The jug gurgles and fills. "I'm done."

Thin Air

The pot gurgles, fills. My head's bourbon-sore.
The sun's a long time clearing this dark out,
Ascending the Santa Ritas before
It shows high and mighty and brings the heat.

He and I clambered up there once, Mt. Wrightson,
Through snow in tee-shirts, at the top a little
Dazed, heaven-drunk, this town only flecks of white.

He gravitated toward it, that thin air,
His whole life, in the broken-winged Corsair,

His first plane; on mountains, Popocatepetl,

Rainier; and perhaps he feels his death that way,
A blue yonder. He believed something there
Looked out for him, and that's all he would say.
Ascents were his high sign, next thing to prayer.

San Xavier del Bac

Ascent. Prayer. Sign. Next thing, I'm on the highway
North. I've felt followed by full moons before;
Trees, once; but never this, not a whole sky,
The whole way to Mission San Xavier.

San Francisco's white coverlet is pinned
With pleas, snapshots, *milagros*, trinket limbs,
Symbols of pain the Saint is asked to mend.

The walls' profusions of figure and color
Stay human; blend pleasure and dolor,

Dance and death; ground their praise though the eye climbs.

God's house has prickly pear in its mortar.
Each candle, someone's grief. Hundreds of them.
I light one for him, the next thing to prayer,
And go back. The whole sky, the whole way home.

Fall

Back home tomorrow. A long way. The whole
Sky snow-dark. Phone calls. Today's not been good,
The effects of one or another pill.
He stammers and fogs, sleeps over his food.

My mother's cough, her back, and her bum knee
Concern me more. The thought she'll be alone,
Day after day; I'm here just six, and *flee*

Is starting to stack up fine next to *fight*.
And I could almost wish an end of it—

A long grief done, her pleasures later on—

If I thought, for all his terror of falling,
That last fall might be his fear's opposite,
Headlong, joyous, as if his one true call
Were his going's soft dream descent through white.

Three Toasts at My Father's Grave

Mid-way through this ritual I've designed—
Drizzling your marker with single-malt scotch—
I stop, with half the flask as yet undrained,
Having pictured you there watching, your pained
Look, your shaking head. "The boy's lost his mind,"
I hear you say. "That belongs down the hatch,
Old buddy, not pissed-away on the ground.
Rotgut I could maybe see; or a blend;
But *that's* the good stuff, and *this* is a ditch
Filled with ashes—though the stone's a nice touch.
So, knock it down. But since you're driving, watch
Yourself." Imagined ghost, no need to bend
A willing arm. I do hereby suspend
This rite and will drink up as you command.

A toast, then, to your neighbors, like you beyond reach
Of whiskey, tears, and toasts, but still: Cleveland,
Moore, Smith, Waldrup, Hutch-
Insons Mr. and Mrs., and of course my own grand-
Parents, I hope you recognize a friend
To this slope, a yearly pilgrim, and won't think I offend
If the tongue naming you is bathed in good hootch.
You are one equal company, the pure and stained,
The poor and (to judge by some of the statuary) rich,
And now that you number my father in the band
Your collective honor is raised a notch,
If only to a nobler grade of mulch.

And a swig for you, Private Vogel, in your stretch
Of ground not ten yards off, the beach-
Sand white of your stone mossing at the top edge
Like cauliflower too long in the fridge.
You were my father's immigrant uncle, who signed
On with Black Jack Pershing in the War to End
All Wars. I wonder whose bullet did you catch?
Townsman's? Teacher's? For his homeland
Was the very same you Vogels abandoned.

Did it give you pause, re-crossing the big pond
On such
An errand?
Not enough to matter, in any case. This niche
Was dug for you before you turned
Twenty, the year your nephew was born. Which

Brings us back around
To the latest tenant of this leaf-littered swatch
Of hillside, this year-old wound
Where they trepanned
The dirt, then bandaged it with this patch
Of granite made to match
Your parents'. We'd make the trip down here each
Memorial Day; you'd stand where I stand
Now, not saying all that much,
And what little you did say leavened
With a laugh about that poor son of a bitch,
The old man, or how you would commit the Dutch
Act before you'd let age keep you pinned
To chairs, homes. Neither maudlin nor thick-skinned,
Your tone, and I've tried here to snatch
A little of that. Your brother, the Reverend
George, would have drawn on a rite more sanctioned
And found words more apt than my stumbling botch.
But perhaps this suits you better, whose faith shunned
The language and liturgies of any church.
And what in this I ought to scratch,
Your good heart, were you here, would silently amend.
That feel for silences should teach
Me now to close, and I do, with a drink and a pledge
To return in the new year. I'll find
You not much changed, I suppose, and be stunned
Again by your death—and by your life, how it can reach
Past these chiseled dates to lend
Its gravity and grace to my own living's pitch
And yaw—for which this was planned
To thank you, but has instead found
Its real meaning to be beyond
Speech.

Dead Letter to a Special Agent

This can't reach you anymore. Nor could you reply,
Having gained your tight-lipped life's apotheosis.
There's no jury so grand that you must testify
To what you know, there where knowing's become *gnosis*.

I see you always in headsets—whether you fire
Rounds at the police range or taxi your small plane
Or sit at the listening end of a tapped wire.

That you listen-in on this is just a child's dream—
But *your* child's, trying to make this new silence seem

What the old one was: love, with nothing to explain.

Nearer the Truth

Perhaps I will say, *The day has broken,*
Or, *The morning has come,* as if
It were merely a matter of sitting here,
Waiting for colors to make their first faint
Pronouncements—

When I know it's not like that, when it's
Nearer the truth to say I've stepped out
To meet it as I always do, mute, barefoot,
Tuning the strings of my attention;
When I, too, have broken, have risen
From the dark and found a horizon; I, too,
Have turned toward the light like a planet.

That's a mystery, I might say, as if
The thing doesn't make its own perfect sense,
Doesn't follow a native logic of neuron
Or simple survival—

When I know that's not true; when it's only
My parting the branches with my question
Or sifting the usual dust when this
Gold appears; when all I'm saying is
I don't know, and any microscope or dog
Could nose-out the plain truth.

If I say of my father that he has *passed,*
It is always *away,* as if distance
Or a new wall were the only truth, now—

When I know that's not how it is at all;
When he goes ahead and I follow,
Admiring, same as ever, only now
He's taken that huge stride straight into

The center of me, into a space
I thought I'd made ready but got wrong.
He's passed *into*, not *away*; to follow
Means seeing myself new, same as ever.

So, I will say, *I have spoken my mind*—
When I know that's not the half of it.
When really I've spoken the cerebellum's
Music and balance, the reptilian brain's
Flickering tongue; spoken my comings-from
And arrivals, my failures to arrive;
Spoken my poured-over pages, my body's
Changes, my question after question;
Spoken this earth I travel, lovingly—yes,
Even that arm's-length shaft dug out of it
Into which I have handed down ashes.

From the Top of Mt. Wrightson

Fifteen hundred feet below and one summit over,
Dead stars flock to an observatory's eggshell dome
To be reborn. The slow, subtle, determined violence
That raised up these peaks, the rock pushing toward sky and stars,

Its aftershock still travels up, trembles my knees now
The way the teacup trembles on its way to your lips,
Your body's dark shiftings toward stone sending up tremors.
The changes still left you will be long years happening;

But from here, where the naked eye makes out the world's curve,
The Santa Rita vertebrae, the Mexico line,
Green pecan groves, your town's rooftops like scattered potshards—
From here even those years grow visible, a distance

Desert-colored, neither earth nor air but as if each
One's prayer to become the other had been smiled upon.
And more than these heights it's that distance unnerving me,
Since crossing it means I'll have arrived at your absence.

Before the airplane, they scanned the slope from here for fires.
A foundation, a small square of square stone, still remains,
Where I sit now looking down toward you—not for fire, but
For some impossible spark from a bracelet or fork

Catching light where you sit at your patio table,
Or a flicker of water tipped from a silver can
Where you go from plant to plant in your slippers, looking
Up once toward me, using your free hand for a hat brim.

But since neither your gaze nor mine ever quite arrives,
I'll have you know that, perched at this abandoned outpost,
The wingbeat of old stars blurring past, I've seen it clear
As a treeline: your going, where the years will give out,

Where they'll leave me with only this way of knowing you,
A welling up, a thermal where the dizzy eye turns.
But for now that won't do, not while these legs can haul me
Back down switchbacks, over patches of snow-covered stone

That must look to you like white flags on the mountainside,
And back down the pine-needled, root-gnarled path, aching, dry;
Not while you're still there laughing like water spilled over,
While the peak surrenders to dark and we can still touch.

If You Lived Here

The return trip was taunted
By railroad crossings, sweet corn stands,
Stacked melons, rooms to be rented
Over the corner dairy; and more than once
A side road, the promise of a distance
Ending in a life I've always wanted.

All for having somewhere else
To be, a life I had to get back to.
I nearly gave in to Bridgeville's
Welcome sign as I was passing through:
If You Lived Here, You'd Be Home Now.
Millville, Seabreeze, Hardscrabble, Federals–

Burg—I longed to be their native.
At the open window, wind slapped
My forearm and billowed my sleeve
Like that white sail, its fat stripe
The orange of ripened cantaloupe,
Crossing the bay as I readied to leave.

But say I buckled, and chose to stay.
Day breaking to the cries of gulls,
The gusts and the wide-open sky,
Would only bring back my son's wails
When he first hit air, and how the walls
Gathered round a new world that day;

Or I'd wake, without you, above
The dairy, to a toy train whistle
Outside, those wooden ones they carve
And sell to tourists—then nestle
Back to a dream: the 12:10 from Newcastle,
On which your letter has said you'll arrive.

Small Ode to My Ignorance

Poets, if they're genuine, must also keep repeating,
'I don't know.'

—WISŁAWA SZYMBORSKA

To wake, at this age, and realize how
Little one knows of so many things—
Who wouldn't feel a bit like a beast,
Concerned with its corner of pasture
Or a master's voice, and little besides?

I speak of the quotidian, the necessary,
The near-to-hand—not the esoterica
Of valences or the mason wasp,
But bridges, say, or the sun, plumbing,
Gluten, flight, the bowels, acoustics,
Wind. Muscle. Money. Anything
Brought to me through cables.

I bat a big eye at these things, I low
At them, then drop my head back
In the bucket and feed.

Love, what does it mean when you ask
About roads and directions, something
So plain as time, and how it is we've
Arrived here and are somehow *for* each
Other, and all I can do for reply is rub
My head against you like the cat?
I'd like to claim my ignorance
Is the very source and ground of all
Hungers, all wanting, that it begins
Any answer I would make you,

But I can say only that I wear it
Like a bell. Whenever I move, whatever
I do, it clatters its summons—at which
The whole stark world of my unknowing
Assembles, right there, beyond me.

On Being Asked, Rhetorically, Where My Next Poem Will Come From

Seeing that you've given me only two
Possible answers—A and B—and B
Is *My clenched ass*, I think I'll go with A:
My free heart. Free to watch the robin build,
As it must, its nest in our lilac tree;
Free to listen as your morning's routine
Rhythms play out—your moan as you sit up
In bed, your foot-slaps on the bathroom floor,
Your lilting questions to the cats about
Their sleep or whether they've been out to play,
Your teacup's knock on the table, the news-
Paper's rustling. Free, in obedience
To its beating's marching orders, to sing—
And not just for supper, but for its life.

Free hearts, free foreheads—that comes from the poem
You laugh at me for having memorized;
Yet there it is, answer A, Ulysses
Praising, as you would, the *frolic welcome*
With which his aging fellow-voyagers
Greet the world. Love, am I not of their tribe,
Getting-on, gray, but knowledge-hungry still?
As to the heart, I know, I know you're right,
You who live the answer to your question.
I would add only this: those mariners'
Asses, though not clenched, are nevertheless
Parked where they need to be, on their benches,
Sitting well in order, ten to a row
And hauling across the *sounding furrows.*

At Frenchman's Bay

for Nin and Jim

Don't come to this coast in your thirties,
With your rocky marriage and second guesses,
Every route in the atlas an exit—

You'll only veer toward some sham freedom
Or higher light, get Jesus-headed, ditch
Verse for the tract or the testament.

Wait till you're fifty or so,
When the dead include some you loved
And you've resigned yourself enough times

To know how to clam-up;
Then you can take in these massive stones,
The vast patience of water, and feel calmed,

Hear millennia lapping at that moment's shore,
The great door thrown open by a wind
Against which the gull both flies and is stilled.

By then you should be ready to step
Between these smaller stones the thicket
Has so obscured you don't, at first, get

Where you're at, until you notice
Human hands set them down here—the rows
Tell you, the spacing; you should have come

Far enough by then to stand among
These nameless markers and scan the bay,
The piled shore, without yearning or dread

Or your mortal pins going wobbly
With loneliness. In your thirties
You'd have started mouthing your loud hymn

To frailty or boyhood,
Raised six bourbons to heaven
And phoned-up your parents in tears—

But not at fifty, and not only because
Those people are gone, like these. By now,
Your going will have learned to be stilled,

To be held in flight, thrown back on itself;
Your quiet, a reply to the ocean's;
Your cry, when it comes, more like a call.

You'll have learned to go back to the house
Without a name for the welcome they've made—
Stone and bay; gull and wind; the dead—

And set a plate on the table, a pot on the stove;
Or pour a slow glass of good whiskey;
Or sit, and set down your syllables in rows.

Photograph © Kelly Bancroft

STEVEN REESE's other titles include *Enough Light to Steer By* (poems, Cleveland State University Press) and, as translator, *Synergos: Selected Poems of Roberto Manzano* (Etruscan Press). His work has appeared widely in periodicals, such as *Poetry Northwest*, *Asheville Poetry Review*, *Green Mountains Review*, and *West Branch*. He lives in Youngstown, Ohio, where he is Professor of English at Youngstown State University and on the faculty of the Northeast Ohio MFA program.